Original title:
Tassels in the Rain

Author: Dexter Sullivan
ISBN HARDBACK: 978-1-80586-210-9
ISBN PAPERBACK: 978-1-80586-682-4

Vibrant Soggy Whirls

Puddles dance with tiny feet,
Colors swirl in laughter sweet.
Raindrops play a game of chase,
Splashing joy in every space.

Umbrellas flip and spin around,
Like mushrooms in a circus found.
Rubber boots parade the street,
Making rainy days a treat.

Ankle-Deep in Colorful Cascades

In boots so bright, I leap and bound,
Through streams that giggle, joys unbound.
A splash here, a splash there too,
I think the sky just laughed at you!

Dancing puddles, wiggly glee,
Swirling skirts, oh, can’t you see?
Each droplet grins, a playful tease,
As colors twist in rainy breeze.

Stormy Adornments at Play

Breezy hats like sails on heads,
Turn a frown to flying spreads.
Kites and giggles whirl around,
As umbrellas take a spin and bound.

Foggy lenses make us gawk,
Sudden slips—a comical walk.
Windswept hair, it’s all a game,
Soggy socks, but who’s to blame?

Drizzled Patterns on Woven Dreams

Rain strokes colors on the ground,
Making puddles that resound.
Every drop a little tease,
Whispers carry on the breeze.

We dance like leaves in swirling air,
Skipping mischief everywhere.
Join the fun in muddy cheer,
Where laughter blooms and dreams appear.

Dances of Fiber and Rain

Threads of bright colors sway,
Dancing joy in the spray.
Twisting, turning, they gleefully play,
Painting puddles in a quirky ballet.

Laughter leaps with each drip,
As fibers take a slippery trip.
Spinning round in a playful whip,
Who knew rain could be such a comic flip?

Accents Against a Teary Sky

Little bits of fabric fly,
As raindrops waltz, oh so spry.
In the gloomy mist, they amplify,
A silly shout, a cheerful sigh.

Fluffy clouds become the stage,
While raindrops act like a sage.
With a wink and a giggle, they engage,
Tickling hearts, breaking the cage.

Chasing Shadows with a Splash

Splashes echo with a cheer,
As fibers chase the clouds near.
With each dart, they make it clear,
Life’s a dance, stick around, my dear!

Raindrops giggle, puddles gleen,
Funky fibers join the scene.
In this game, we’re all so keen,
Chasing laughter, bright and clean.

Nature’s Embroidered Celebration

In a whirl of colors bright,
Nature throws a fun-filled night.
With each raindrop, a spark of light,
Stitching joy in fibers’ flight.

A chorus of grass makes a tune,
While raindrops waltz beneath the moon.
They play tricks, like a fun cartoon,
Celebrating life in a raucous swoon.

Fringes of a Storm

When clouds wear their gray coats,
And puddles start to laugh,
A mischievous breeze plays tricks,
Chasing hats down the path.

Raindrops cling to playful strands,
Bouncing off the ground,
A soggy dance of hilarity,
Echoes all around.

Whispering Threads on Puddle's Edge

In the hush of a rainy day,
Threads talk in the wet,
Glances slip and slide away,
Like a comedy duet.

A duck quacks with great delight,
As water splashes high,
Catching glimmers of the light,
Beneath a moody sky.

Beads of Water and Woven Dreams

Beads of water, shiny bright,
Decorate each shoe,
With every step, a squishy sound,
A symphony so true.

And as the rain starts to waltz,
A puddle-perfect scene,
We prance through nature's art,
Like kids who are quite keen.

Dance of the Drenched Finery

In coats that shimmer, wet and bold,
We sway to nature's beat,
With splashes as our music score,
Each twirl, a drippy treat.

Umbrellas spinning like a kite,
Lift dreams above the ground,
As laughter joins the grand parade,
In this wet joy we've found.

Liquid Tresses in Motion

Bouncing curls that twirl and sway,
Dancing down the street today.
Umbrellas bounce like rubber ducks,
Catching laughter, dodging muck.

Drenched shoes squeak, a silly sound,
While giggles echo all around.
Some splash in puddles, hearts so light,
In this clownish, drenched delight.

Hats fly high, a wild parade,
As rain turns joy to a masquerade.
Oh, the mess we gladly greet,
In this soggy, jolly feat.

Threads of Joy in the Deluge

Jumpy rain and silly shoes,
A splash of water, what a muse!
Bright colors swirl in nature's play,
While giggling kids decide to stay.

Each puddle pops like happy corn,
As laughter breaks upon the morn.
Coats party hard, they spin and whirl,
A shower curtain with a twirl.

Wet socks are grand, a fashion show,
As lightning strikes a funny glow.
We wear our wetness with high glee,
Dancing joyously, wild and free.

Shimmering Below the Clouds

Raindrops cling to noses bright,
Like jewels glistening in the light.
Running, slipping, what a sight,
Laughter echoes, pure delight!

Floppy hats and muddied heels,
We're all just children with big appeals.
The sky spills fun, a comic brew,
As giggles rise with each wide view.

Snappy jokes and drippy hair,
Splashing rain becomes our flair.
Jumping as the waters fly,
Chasing laughter, oh so spry!

The Brightness After the Storm

As wet furrows dry in sun,
Silly faces share the fun.
Rainbows grin across the sky,
Each giggle now a butterfly.

We shake the raindrops from our coats,
Like champs with soggy little boats.
Weathered giggles gather light,
In puddles deep, we find our flight.

Clouds roll back to show their cheer,
With every laugh, the world is clear.
So here we stand, heads high in sun,
Celebrating storms, oh what fun!

Rich Threads Beneath a Grey Veil

A flower pot scoots away,
Its dance is quite absurd today.
With puddles gleaming, it twirls with glee,
Chasing raindrops like it's flying free.

A cat in boots jumps to the side,
Hating how the rain has lied.
It shakes its paw with utmost flair,
Wishing for sunshine, warm and rare.

A squirrel spins in a splashy trot,
Grabbing acorns, giving it all a shot.
Each droplet holds a giggle, quite,
In stormy weather, it’s pure delight.

Laughter echoes through the street,
With umbrellas turned upside down, oh what a treat!
Dancing in puddles, they leap and sway,
In this wet jest, joy leads the way.

Shimmering Fringes in the Downpour

When the clouds decide to play,
Everything turns into a cabaret.
Jacket sleeves flapping, so absurd,
As raindrops fall with a silly urge.

Footwear squishes with each bold step,
While umbrellas duel, oh what a prep!
The wind gives hats a humorous fling,
Sorting out chaos—it's a grand thing.

A toddler shrieks, leaves joyfully,
Worms parade it—oh, look at me!
Splashes send giggles through the air,
Funny moments beyond compare.

With raincoats bright in flippy spin,
The river of laughter flows from within.
As clouds melt down their lively glare,
We twirl in puddles without a care.

Dappled Colors in a Wet Embrace

Splashes of joy paint the ground,
In this downpour, silliness is found.
Rain boots kick up a vibrant show,
Waltzing puddles as laughter flows.

A dog in shades strikes a pose,
Dashing 'round in laughter's throes.
Bouncing droplets become the scene,
Transforming gray to a jolly green.

Chasing rainbows amidst the mess,
Each giggle feels like sweet success.
With every drop a chuckle hides,
Fun erupts as the water slides.

Dripping hearts across the way,
In this wet wonder, we choose to play.
Life's joy blooms, even soaked in grace,
While colors swirl in this embrace.

Vivid Hues in the Storm's Caress

As the heavens join the fun,
Puddles mirror the hinting sun.
Strangers laugh, umbrellas collide,
In this crazy dance, smiles reside.

Faces soaked yet spirits bright,
Embrace the rain with sheer delight.
A pop of color to every drip,
Joy flows freely in the friendship quip.

Children leap with crafty flair,
Wildly splashing without a care.
Their laughter sings through stormy skies,
Adding magic where fun lies.

So, let the clouds drench us in cheer,
For vivid hues draw the fun near.
In each tiny drop, joy resides,
As life's laughter in the rain abides.

Twirls in the Shadow of Clouds

Dancing while droplets fall,
A puddle's call, a funny brawl.
Umbrellas flip, a wild sway,
We twirl and giggle, come what may.

Footwear squelches, does a jig,
Wiggling toes, oh so big!
Clouds chuckle, watching us play,
In this joyful, drizzly ballet.

Slick streets reflect our bright cheer,
Such silly sights from far and near.
With each slip, laughter does grow,
A rain-drenched comedy show!

We leap and splatter, full of zest,
In wet chaos, we are blessed.
So let it pour, we feel no shame,
Each splash becomes a wacky game.

Drenched Elegance in Motion

Raindrops wear a tux and tie,
As we glide and slip awry.
Sassy spins in oversize shoes,
Who knew being wet was such good news?

A walrus waltzes past a tree,
With hats and coats, oh what a spree!
Drenched elegance, we think we're grand,
But then we meet the slippery land.

Chasing puddles, what a chase,
Covered in mud, oh what a face!
Dripping style is all the rage,
As we perform on this wet stage.

Each slip is met with howling glee,
'Is that a dance?' they ask with glee.
With giggles loud, we'll strut and prance,
In this rain-soaked, silly dance!

Cloudy Patterns Overflowing with Life

In the gray, we paint the floor,
With every splash, we're wanting more.
A splash of joy, a flip of glee,
Nature's canvas, wild and free.

Watch the rain, it's learning to dance,
Bouncing bubbles in a playful prance.
A paper boat sails with a wink,
Its cargo full of dreams to think.

We wave to skies, they wink back bright,
As puddles sparkle in soft twilight.
With outfits soaked in colors loud,
We stomping, laughing, feeling proud.

So in this storm, let laughter rise,
Wit and wisdom beneath gray skies.
For every drop has a story to tell,
In patterns alive, we laugh so well.

Ribbons of Color Beneath Raindrops

Colors ribbons in the sky,
Frolic as the raindrops fly.
Swoosh and swirl, we splash around,
Giggling echoes, a joyful sound.

A slip of green, a dash of blue,
Each hue dancing, can you see too?
With each raindrop, we come alive,
A silly swim where we all thrive.

Puddles grin, reflecting light,
Sock puppets wave, what a sight!
With laughter loud, we chart our way,
Through this vibrant, funny display.

Clouds conspire, rain's the game,
We leap and bound, no fear, no shame.
For ribbons of color may fade away,
But joy in the rain is here to stay!

Lacy Cascades in a Shimmering Shower

Raindrops dance on strings like threads,
Creating laughter in puddles, they tread.
Wet umbrellas bob like ducks at play,
As giggles echo—come join the fray!

Fringes flutter, embracing the breeze,
Jumping to move with amusing ease.
Raincoats parade in colors so bright,
While puddles splash under streetlamp's light.

With every drip, a new prank unfolds,
Backyard rivers where mischief beholds.
Slipping and sliding, they laugh and squeal,
In this rainy circus, joy is surreal.

So grab your coat and don't you delay,
In this playful storm, come out and sway.
The world's a stage, with laughter we'll reign,
In our lacy cascades, let's dance in the rain!

Radiant Flickers Beneath the Overcast

Clouds gather like a fluffy brigade,
As excitement builds for the splash parade.
Dancing droplets, a tap on the cheek,
Amusing antics feel lively and cheeky.

Colors burst forth like confetti rained,
Splish-splashing stomps keep spirits unchained.
A sneaky splash from a playful friend,
In this drenched delight, the fun won’t end.

Vivid umbrellas paint the gray sky,
While giggling puddles give reasons to fly.
With each sideways glance, laughter ignites,
As we dodge the showers, scaling new heights.

Lively flickers of laughter take flight,
In this downpour, let’s relish the night.
So, join the fun and skip like a sprite,
Under the overcast, everything feels bright!

Rhythm of the Rain on Fabric's Curve

Raindrops tap dance on every tier,
With a whimsical beat, they bring us cheer.
Draped in fabric, our outfits will sway,
Wriggling and giggling, we laugh all day.

Soggy socks hold secrets in their fold,
While laughter bubbles up, stories unfold.
Running wild, we collect little streams,
Building a castle of whimsical dreams.

A patchwork of patterns that tickles the eye,
Umbrellas become parachutes in the sky.
As clotheslines sag with laughter's sweet tunes,
We sway to the rhythm, beneath drizzly moons.

So let the fabric flow, let giggles unspool,
In this rain-washed playground, we dance like a fool.
With every drop, joy's measures will curve,
In the rhythm of laughter, our hearts will serve!

Iridescent Tales in the Midst of Pour

In the midst of showers, a tale takes flight,
With raindrops giggling in pure delight.
Rubber boots splatter, making a scene,
As we dance in puddles, all cheerful and keen.

The sky dons a coat of thick, moody gray,
But our vibrant spirits won’t fade away.
Colors shimmer through water and light,
In this rain-soaked adventure, we take our height.

A splash leads to laughter; it's a slippery draw,
With each waterfall, comes a new silly flaw.
Umbrellas, like mushrooms, spring from the ground,
In our iridescent tale, joy truly abounds.

So gather your friends, let the levy break,
In this playful downpour, we’ll make laughter quake.
With tales of delight, let the rain gently pour,
Together we’ll shine, in the midst of the roar!

Chasing Drizzles with Fanciful Hues

Puddles dance in painted shoes,
Hats tipped low, we skip the blues.
Laughing at the splashes made,
Umbrellas twirl like grand parades.

Giggling as the clouds conspire,
Dancing in a downpour choir.
Once more we splash, we leap, we play,
Around the puddles, come what may.

Rainbows slip on water slides,
Chasing drizzles, joy abides.
Every drop a cheeky grin,
In this water’s playful spin.

So let's embrace the playful tease,
Where raindrops tickle, swirl, and squeeze.
With fanciful hues, we'll laugh and play,
In this rainy world, we'll find our way.

Golden Foams on Glistening Fabrics

Bubbles popping on the street,
Golden foams beneath our feet.
We wear our laughter like a coat,
Slipping on our soggy boat.

Creeping slowly through the mist,
Every splash—an unplanned twist.
Brightly colored shoes do shine,
As we trip on thoughts divine.

Dancing lightly, skirts will fly,
Soaked spaghetti in the sky.
With glistening fabrics all around,
Each step a silly, squishy sound.

So, let us laugh and chase the zany,
In golden foams, life's just so brainy.
As we frolic with joyful cheers,
We'll welcome puddles, banish fears.

Cascades of Color in the Downpour

Cascades tumble, bright and bold,
Turning sidewalks into gold.
A splash of laughter in the rain,
Doughnut hats and socks of grain.

Colors swirl in swirling streams,
Umbrellas float like silly dreams.
We dodge the drops, it's quite a game,
With every shiver, we feel the flame.

Painted rainbows on our cheeks,
Splashes echo with joyful squeaks.
We prance and leap, no time for cold,
Wrapped up in stories yet untold.

So bring your colors to the show,
Let cascades make our spirits glow.
In this downpour, we'll be bright,
With all our glee, we'll win the fight.

Raindrops and Ribbons of Hope

Raindrops play on window sills,
Ribbons dance atop the hills.
With each droplet, a new surprise,
Grinning wide, the laughter flies.

Slips and trips on wobbly streams,
Sneezy giggles fuel our dreams.
In this wacky, rainy maze,
We'll spin together in a daze.

Colorful puddles catch our song,
As we trip, and then say, "No wrong!"
With each splash, our worries fade,
In raindrops, our joy cascades.

So come dear friend, let us entwine,
With ribbons bright and muddy wine.
In the laughter of the rain,
We'll weave the magic, shed the pain.

Twilight Emblems in the Rain

Puddles dance like happy feet,
Under cloudy skies they meet.
Umbrellas spin, a playful sight,
As raindrops fall, oh what a delight!

Every splash a giggly tune,
Splashing faces like a cartoon.
Rubber ducks parade in style,
Grinning widely, all the while.

Raincoats flapping, laughter flies,
Chasing rainbows in disguise.
With each drip, a smile blooms,
A jolly scene in nature's rooms.

So let it pour, let’s not complain,
For joy is found in every rain.
In twilight's glow, we skip and sing,
As puddles mirror the joy we bring.

The Rainbow's Serenade in Wet Winds

Whirling winds with a breezy cheer,
Splashes of color draw us near.
A serenade from clouds above,
As giggles rain down like a dove.

Kites get tangled, oh what a mess,
Kids with giggles, embracing the stress.
Dodging raindrops like dodgeball champs,
Crowning puddles with dreamy stamps.

Wet socks squelch, a funny sound,
Skipping in circles, round and round.
No worries here about the gloom,
For laughter breaks the raindrop's doom.

In colors bright, we'll dance and sway,
Chasing shadows, come what may.
Beneath gray skies, adventures bloom,
In this whimsical, joyful room.

Enchanted Strands Under a Soaked Sky

Beaded bubbles on kids' heads,
Swaying strands like silly threads.
Giggling friends, they jump and play,
In splashes bright, they mold their day.

A hat becomes a boat afloat,
Sending sailors on a joke-filled note.
Laughter echoes, splatter, splash,
As tiny feet make the puddles crash.

Sopping wet from head to toe,
Yet spirits rise, they steal the show.
Each droplet whispers secrets sweet,
In a world where fun and laughter meet.

So grab your pals and take the plunge,
In laughter's arms, let's all indulge.
For under skies that seem to weep,
We find our joy, our hearts will leap.

Fluid Vignettes of Nature’s Palette

Dancing colors paint the scene,
Every drop a painter's dream.
Splashes tell a tale so bright,
In this storm, we take flight.

Colors swirl, a crazy sight,
Wet shoes squeak, oh what a fright!
With every swirl and every twirl,
Life’s a canvas, make it whirl!

Pailfuls of laughter in the air,
Sticky fingers, messy hair.
As rainbows form in the misty light,
Even clouds can’t hold the delight.

So come on out, don’t be shy,
Let your worries float up high.
In this playful nature’s mix,
We find our joy, our silly tricks.

Inspiration in Every Drop

Puddles form like art displays,
With squishy shoes and wet bouquets.
Bright colors splash in joyful cheer,
As clouds above just disappear.

Umbrellas flip like acrobats,
While ducks parade in fancy hats.
Raindrops dance upon my nose,
The sky winks down, as humor grows.

Shining Fringes Beneath the Storm

Beneath the clouds, we prance about,
Like goofy kids, we dance and shout.
Winds a-whirling, laughter flies,
As raindrops play their sweet surprise.

Cool breezes tickle silly dreams,
While rivers laugh, or so it seems.
Each splash a giggle, each drop a song,
We skip along, where we belong.

Cascade of Colors on Wet Surface

The world’s a palette, bright and bold,
With colors mixed, a sight to behold.
Jumping in, a squishy delight,
As rainbows burst in splashes bright.

We twirl and swirl through puddles deep,
Each footstep sends the colors leap.
Oh, how we giggle, as we slip,
A carnival ride, on friendship's trip.

Musical Notes in a Rainy Glow

Each drop that falls, a playful beat,
Dancing on rooftops, oh so sweet.
Piano keys in puddled streams,
Sing songs of laughter, twist our dreams.

With every splash, a rhythm found,
Soaked and silly, we spin around.
The world's our stage, the rain our tune,
In this soggy dance, we're over the moon!

Silk and Water: A Poetic Collision

With a flip and a flop, they sway,
Dancing droplets, here to play.
A sassy spin in puddles bright,
Silken threads in pure delight.

Bubbles burst with joyous grace,
Glistening drops begin the race.
Oh, the mischief they create,
Tangled laughter, never late!

Poised Frills in the Heart of Thunder

Oh, the frills of life in stormy airs,
They float and twirl without a care.
While thunder grumbles, silk takes flight,
Waving hello to a gloomy night.

Each gust a giggle, loud and bright,
Frills on a journey, pure delight.
In downpour's embrace, they laugh and shout,
Stormy ballet, without a doubt!

Whispers of Drenched Threads

Whispers of fabric in the rain,
Telling secrets, voicing pain.
Yet in each droplet, a chuckle hides,
As threads giggle, their worries subside.

Under clouds, they dream and snicker,
Twisting with water, just a flicker.
Laughing stitches play their tune,
Drenched in joy, beneath the moon!

Raindrops on Fringe

Raindrops play on fringes fine,
Bouncing merrily, how they shine!
Each little plop, a silly sound,
Sassy frills twirl round and round.

As puddles form, they jump right in,
Giggles echo, let games begin.
Wet and wild, they frolic free,
Fringes laughing, what a spree!

Seaside Fringes Dancing in Drops

At the shore, the colors play,
Fringes swaying, come what may.
Gulls join in with silly shouts,
As laughter spills from happy mouths.

Waves crash down in a rhythmic beat,
Catching everyone off their feet.
With wild hats and shoes askew,
We dance around like fish, who knew?

Sunshine peeks through a silver gray,
A comical scene of hip hooray.
As droplets spin, we can't refrain,
From giggling hard amidst the rain.

Barefoot moments full of cheer,
Splashing puddles, we have no fear.
With friends around, we all proclaim,
This rainy seaside is our game!

The Umbrella of Woven Hues

An umbrella bright, in colors vast,
We twirl and sway, forget the past.
Covered from drops, we still don’t care,
For laughter echoes in the air.

Friends gather close beneath the dome,
With quirky jokes, we feel at home.
A splash of rain and a little dance,
Gives ordinary days a funny chance.

We sing to clouds, share silly tales,
Imitating each other's flails.
With guests of honor, the raindrops fall,
Each splash a hi-five, a cannonball!

Through woven shades, we peek and grin,
Here’s to the fun that’s lurking within.
Though skies may frown, our hearts stay bright,
Under this rainbow, all’s just right!

Rippling Tangles and Raindrop Splashes

From the sky, the raindrops fling,
They dance like little, joyful things.
Frogs croak a tune, on lily pads,
While kids spin round in their own fads.

Rippling water, quick and sly,
Catching giggles as they fly.
With every splash, a tiny cheer,
Let's muddle up these funny fears!

Hats go flying, hair a mess,
But puddles bring us happiness.
In wobbly lines, the ducklings stomp,
Creating ripples, a perfect rom-com.

We twirl in circles, laughter wide,
In this silly downpour, we slide.
For raindrop splashes can't be beat,
With laughter echoing, we can't retreat!

Raindrop Adornments on Life’s Fabric

Life's fabric glistens, beads of cheer,
Each raindrop adds a shiny sphere.
With patches of fun sewn here and there,
We stitch together a lively flair.

Umbrella hats and woolly socks,
Dance around like goofy clocks.
Spinning raindrops in a mixed dance,
We gather joy in whimsical chance.

Every droplet, a memory bright,
In this wild storm, we hold on tight.
We swap the plan for joyous glee,
As laughter spills in harmony.

So raise a glass to this rainy spree,
For life’s adornments set us free.
With every splash and every cheer,
Our hearts stay warm amid the drear!

Veils of Mist Over Vivid Trimmings

In puddles deep, the colors dance,
A splash of laughter, a froggy prance.
With every drip, a giggle's sound,
As raindrops play on trimmings found.

The wind's a jester, swirling around,
Tickling edges, where joy is unbound.
A hat gone wild, then swept away,
Makes us chuckle on this gray day.

Bright ribbons twirl, as if in a race,
Their playful tug, a light-hearted chase.
We step and skip through the misty cheer,
Twirling in symphony, free from all fear.

So let the showers bring us delight,
With each puddle jump, we soar to new height.
With veils of mist, our spirits take flight,
As laughter echoes, a colorful sight.

Shimmering Accents Beneath Gray Skies

Under clouds, like paint on a scene,
A handful of sparkles, a silly routine.
A twinkle here, a wink from the rain,
Who knew gray days held such sweet gain?

Layers shimmer, like laughter on lips,
With every raindrop, a little eclipse.
A parade of puddles, we whimsically leap,
As dapper leaves in their soggy heap.

A caper of colors, a comic parade,
With umbrellas spinning, and no plans laid.
As gray skies chuckle, our spirits ignite,
With quicksilver joy, we dance through the night.

In a flash, the sun makes a guesty debut,
And glimmering accents find life, bright and new.
We'll laugh with the raindrops, shake off the gloom,
For beneath cloudy skies, there’s always room!

Lush Layers Swirl in Wet Whispers

A cascade of layers, soft and bright,
Spin with a giggle, in morning light.
Wet whispers tickle, as smiles unfold,
With frolicsome layers, more laughter than gold.

Each splash reveals a secret unseen,
A leaping dance, where fun reigns supreme.
With soggy socks, we leap and run,
In this playful world, there's never a shun.

Round we go, as the skies contribute,
A joyful symphony, where laughter's our flute.
We're merry pranksters, a jolly brigade,
Sailing through puddles, as if we'd paraded.

So let the wet whispers serenade our play,
As we weave through the chaos of this rainy ballet.
With lush layers swirling, our hearts find the cheer,
In every drenching laugh, bright spirits appear.

Liquid Prisms Embrace the Embellishments

Beneath the splatter, a rainbow's show,
Liquid prisms glistening, oh what a glow!
We dance through the droplets like feathery sprites,
Wearing raindrop jewels, such wonderful sights!

With every splash, the giggles abound,
A whimsical world where joy can be found.
Our clothes gaudy splashes, our shoes all a mess,
In this merry dance, we need not impress.

Embellishments dripping, we twirl through the spray,
With each little giggle, we chase gloom away.
Our laughter a tapestry, woven with cheer,
As liquid light ripples, brightening near.

So gather your whimsy and let it unfold,
In this joyous journey, be daring, be bold.
For when rain meets laughter, and splashes take flight,
We'll paint a new canvas, in pure delight!

Glorious Droplets in Motion

Splashes dance on rooftops bright,
Like little shoes in a playful fight.
Umbrellas bob, a curious sight,
As puddles giggle under the light.

Children leap, a joyful spree,
Splashing water, oh what glee!
Raincoats flap, like birds set free,
While waddling ducks just sip their tea.

Fringed Reflections on a Puddle

Mirrors shiver, the ground adorned,
With wisps of laughter, all unworn.
Wellington boots, all shiny and horned,
Creating ripples, where dreams are spawned.

Clouds play peek-a-boo, so sly,
Trying to make us wave goodbye.
As rain drops curtain off the sky,
We stomp and splash, oh my, oh my!

Rain-Kissed Pendants of Color

Raindrops hang like candy bright,
On leaves that twirl in sheer delight.
A splash of joy, a little fight,
As puddles dress in hues of light.

Silly hats on heads so round,
Catch a drop and spin around.
Jokes are shared without a sound,
In this wet circus, laughs abound!

The Raindrop Embellishment

Jewel-like beads on window sills,
Perform a dance, oh what a thrill!
With every drop, the laughter spills,
As nature's voice, our hearts it fills.

Puddles pop, like bubbles in flight,
A serenade in gloomy light.
With each splash, our hearts ignite,
As happiness blooms, annoying the night.

Fluttering Hues Amidst Nature’s Tears

Colors dance and sway,
Chasing droplets all day.
They giggle as they gleam,
In puddles, they all beam.

Bright shades take a spin,
In the chaos, they grin.
With each splash, a cheer,
Who knew rain could bring cheer?

A whirl of joy around,
In the puddles, joy is found.
Each hue finds a friend,
In the laughter, they blend.

With a twirl and a dip,
Through raindrops, they skip.
Nature's brush strokes come alive,
As the colors twist and jive.

Watching Colors Bleed in the Downpour

When the skies start to cry,
Colors twirl up and fly.
As they merge and collide,
Oh, what a joyful ride!

They drip and they leak,
A comedy unique.
Washing streets with hues bright,
Splashing joy left and right.

Amidst the gloomy gray,
They find a wacky play.
With every thunder roar,
Colors dance, and skies soar.

Giggling as they fall,
They answer nature's call.
For in every single drop,
A rainbow does a hop!

Warmth of Stitching in Chilling Showers

Needles play in the rain,
Crafting warmth from the pain.
With each stitch, laughter grows,
As fabric sways and flows.

Wool and cotton combine,
In the storm, they intertwine.
Creating warmth with flair,
In the chill, a fashion dare!

As pattern fights the gloom,
Threaded jokes start to bloom.
Each knit is a giggle,
In the rain, they all wiggle.

In a world turned to gray,
Colors bright come to play.
With a snicker and a tease,
They spin in the breeze!

Enchanted Patterns Caught in a Deluge

Patterns twirl like a dance,
Caught up in the rain's prance.
Each drop brings a new chance,
To join in the wild romance.

In the chaos, they swirl,
Their edges start to unfurl.
With each splash, a new cheer,
Crafting magic far and near.

They giggle as they glide,
Through puddles, they do slide.
As the shower sings loud,
Patterns form a playful crowd.

In this joyous retreat,
Every drop feels so sweet.
Among the playful rains,
Their laughter always reigns.

Spirals of Drenched Elegance

In puddles, they dance, oh what a sight,
As splashes of joy take flight.
Their colors twirl with pure delight,
Making the gloomy feel just right.

Raindrops tickle as they glide,
Like playful jests that can’t hide.
Each twist and turn, a wild ride,
A jumbled mess that smiles wide.

So when the clouds parade their gray,
These swirling threads come out to play.
With laughter loud in their ballet,
They turn the tempest into sway.

Now behold this drenched display,
Where chaos reigns and giggles stay.
With storms on stage, we make our way,
In spirals bright that won’t betray.

Lush Threads Beneath Stormy Skies

Beneath the clouds, a vibrant show,
Lush fibers sprout, how they glow!
In droplets, they giggle and flow,
As blustery winds put on their show.

Umbrellas flip in comical grace,
While drenched folks slip in this race.
Nature's laughter, a witty pace,
Every little splash a cozy embrace.

With every drip, the fun unfolds,
Adventures bright, brave hearts bold.
Dancing threads, like stories told,
In storms, our merriment takes hold.

So romp and play, ignore the frown,
Let laughter drench you, don't drown!
In this lush whirl, you wear the crown,
As clouds above turn upside down.

A Soaked Canvas of Life's Threads

A canvas splashed with colors bright,
As raindrops paint in sheer delight.
Threads soaked through, a comical sight,
Life's messy craft, oh what a fright!

Winds swirl like jesters, play their jest,
While soggy socks have quite the quest.
Each bead of water proves it's best,
As giggles burst, we feel so blessed.

In puddles deep, our laughter skips,
With every fall, we take new trips.
Jumping high, it's laughter's whips,
The wetness drawing silly quips.

So here's to fun in drops galore,
To life's wet canvas and much more.
In every squish, there's room to soar,
With threads so soaked, we all adore!

Garlands of Water and Whimsy

Garlands made of laughing streams,
As whimsy flows in every dream.
Caught in the rain, we dance and beam,
In puddles swift, we chase the gleam.

Each raindrop sings a silly song,
As carpets of wetness dance along.
We jump around, where we belong,
In water’s grip, we all grow strong.

With every splash, a story grows,
As laughter spills, it surely shows.
In this wild downpour, joy bestows,
A tapestry where friendship glows.

So let the skies let loose their fun,
Together we laugh, a crazy run.
Under the clouds, our races spun,
Garlands bright while storms are done.

Swaying in the Downpour

Bobbing heads in puddles wide,
Umbrellas flipped, there's nowhere to hide.
Rubber ducks are quacking loud,
Dancing like a dizzy crowd.

Pants are soaked, but spirits high,
Splashes made as we all fly.
Laughing more at each wild wave,
Who knew the rain could be so brave?

Raindrops fall like jiggly treats,
Feet are squishy, can’t find our seats.
Clouds are grumpy, fussing away,
Yet here we are, in playful sway.

Echoes of giggles, a thunderous cheer,
Strangers join in; the weather's a dear.
Dancing drizzles, let’s paint the town,
Swaying about like kings with a crown.

Colors Running Wild

Painted skies, a splatter spree,
Wellies worn like artful tea.
Rainbows tiptoe on the street,
Colors splashed in squishy feat.

With every droplet, hues collide,
A sideways blush, we cannot bide.
Grumpy clouds become our muse,
Creating with these drippy hues.

Lemon drops and cherry cheer,
Umbrella giggles far and near.
Streaks of blue and splats of red,
A canvas formed, where giggles spread.

Messy masterpiece on a rainy day,
Join the fun, don't hide away!
When skies turn gray, let colors sing,
In our art, we find our fling.

Woven Dreams Under Grey Skies

Under clouds that twist and twirl,
In our raincoat caps, we swirl.
Dizzy dreams on a drippy day,
Inviting all, come out to play.

Mismatched socks dance like sprites,
Spinning through those puddle bites.
Twirling round in playful jeers,
Woven tales whispered in our ears.

Kite strings flutter in the mist,
Flying high, none can resist.
Weather winks with a jokester's grin,
While we laugh with the world within.

Wet shoes squeak like happy mice,
Sloshing laughter, no need to think twice.
Under these skies with joy as our guide,
Woven dreams are where we abide.

Adornments in the Mist

Beads of water wink at me,
As I splash and giggle with glee.
Glistening on a drizzly crown,
These fajitas, not a frown!

Donuts spun like clouds above,
Raindrops fall with a dash of love.
Each puddle's a mirror, I spin around,
In this jester's joy, I am crowned.

Silly hats with feathers bright,
Drenched in laughter, pure delight.
We catch the rain like frenetic sprites,
Dancing through our rainy rights.

Each ripple tells a joke anew,
Life's a circus, try not to stew.
With every drop, we twirl with grace,
Adornments found in this splashy place.

Glimmering in the Wet Glow

Droplets dance on my new hat,
Splashing colors where I'm at.
Every step a goofy slide,
With puddles now my joy and glide.

My shoes squeak with every hop,
Like rubber ducks that never stop.
Umbrellas twirl, a wobbly sight,
We dance as if we're light as light.

Raindrops tickle, laughter's free,
Splashing giggles, just like me.
We twirl in puddles, don’t you see?
A festival of rain, whee!

With soggy socks and wild grins,
Each raindrop holds a world of spins.
A carnival of silly pride,
Who knew rain could be such a ride?

Fluttering in the Monsoon

Banners wave in the humid breeze,
Drenched confetti from the trees.
I twirl my raincoat, superhero flair,
Who needs a dry day? I don't care!

Water balloons fly from above,
A water fight, oh what fun to shove!
Neighbors laugh, we sneak and prance,
Chasing rain like a wild dance.

Rubber chickens squawk in glee,
As umbrellas turn into a weird sea.
With every gust, we leap and glide,
The monsoon's joy is our joy ride.

Giggles echo through the street,
While drenching friends feels so sweet.
Wet socks squish, we'll never complain,
In this wild shower, we're all insane!

Cascades of Fabric Dreams

Bright scarves swirl in the chaotic wind,
A colorful whirlwind, laughter pinned.
My raincoat flaps like a wayward kite,
As I bounce through puddles, oh what a sight!

Brightly patterned umbrellas collide,
In this fabric storm we fully abide.
Each step a splash, the joy’s contagious,
We’re drenched yet merry, totally outrageous.

Dresses twirl like dervishes bold,
Every drop a story, waiting to unfold.
Wading through puddles with glee, we shout,
Fabric dreams like a wild rout!

In this silly splash of cloth and rain,
We're all just kids, ignoring the pain.
With every flick, a smile beams,
Cascades of fun, in fabric dreams!

Strands of Hope Amidst Clouds

Clouds grumble but we just grin,
Playing hide and seek with thunder's din.
Our funky hats take flight on the breeze,
Only to land on dancing trees.

Rain drops down like playful tricks,
A splash parade, oh how it clicks!
With paper boats we set afloat,
Racing dreams, no need to gloat.

Jacket pockets filled with glee,
With snacks, laughter, and jelly beans.
Every drizzle brings a cheer,
What's a little rain? Nothing to fear!

So let the skies pour out their pluck,
In puddles deep, let's trudge and luck.
Strands of hope shine bright and wide,
In this funny shower, we all abide!

Colors Drip from the Hem of Twilight

In twilight's glow, colors collide,
Like paint splatters, they giggle and slide.
Each hue a story, bright and bizarre,
Dancing around like a lunar bazaar.

Purple polka dots chasing the blue,
While orange spirals yell, "Look at me too!"
As the sky spills laughter on rooftops and trees,
Making rainbows out of puddles with ease.

But watch out below, where splashes are made,
And umbrellas turn into a clown parade.
The drizzles come down with a ticklish cheer,
Painting the world in colors austere!

So grab your galoshes, forget about gray,
Join jigs and swirls in this vibrant ballet.
For every drop brings a giggle anew,
In twilight's embrace, we dance like we grew.

Elegance Adrift in Silver Showers

In showers of silver, the world gets a soak,
With every drop, elegance laughs and bespoke.
Raindrops like diamonds fall from the sky,
Creating a spectacle that catches the eye.

Dressed in drizzle, the ladies all spin,
Their dresses twirling with a shimmer and grin.
A waltz in the puddles, oh what a sight,
As ducks take the stage in their fancy fright.

A tip of the hat to the stylish raincoat,
With a splashy umbrella, they all seem afloat.
The breeze carries laughter, the joy multiplies,
In this silver dance, let your worries all fry.

So slip on your galoshes, embrace all the fun,
Let elegance waddle, till the day is all done.
In these silver showers, we twirl and we sway,
Adrift in a giggle, come join the ballet!

Glistening Strands Untamed by the Storm

From the windswept turf, there’s a comical sight,
Glistening strands flowing wild in the night.
Laughing like maniacs, they dance in a whirl,
As if hairdos were tossed in a funky old curl.

Bearded men prance with their mops in the rain,
Each strand a rebel, refusing to feign.
With soggy confetti, they wobble and sway,
Laughter erupts as they pull off ballet.

Kites caught in hedges, looking quite mad,
Whispering secrets that make their folks glad.
The storm may be fierce, but oh what a show,
As strands march together, all wild in a row.

So let the rain pour, bring chaos we love,
With each splash, we rise like the stars from above.
In a world where strands flutter, freedom they find,
Untamed by the storm, they weave love intertwined.

Threads of Joy Weave Through Cold Rain

In cold rain's embrace, joy starts to thread,
With giggles like bubbles, they dance overhead.
Raindrops keep stitching the fabric of day,
While puddles erupt with a splash in the fray.

Soggy socks squish as the children all cheer,
Building mud castles, no hint of a fear.
Laughter and splatters blend here in a rush,
As umbrellas tip over, creating a hush.

With threads of delight, they skip and they twirl,
As puddles become portals in a slippery whirl.
Cold rain brings warmth wrapped in fun all around,
In a quilt of pure laughter, joy knows no bound.

So let every storm bring a splash of delight,
Woven adventures, from morning 'til night.
In threads of sweet joy, we'll frolic and play,
With the rain as our partner, we dance all the way.

Rainbow Threads in a Liquid World

Puddles dance with shining hues,
Mud pies in the fading blues.
Socks soaked through, a joyful cheer,
Splashing laughter far and near.

Raindrops tap like tiny drums,
With each hop, a belly thrum.
Colors mix in crazy ways,
Dancing in the rainy haze.

The Soft Tones of a Rainy Night

Raindrops whisper on the street,
Until the thunder gives a beat.
Umbrellas twirl like dancing hats,
As cats give out their soggy rants.

Moonlight slips through fluffy gray,
Watching all the splashes play.
Piano keys beneath the gloom,
Turn raindrops into silly tunes.

Anthems of Hanging Threads

Overhangs get their playful vibe,
Where laughter takes a funny jibe.
Kites get tangled in the breeze,
Like shoelaces tied with ease.

Colors twine in a flimsy dance,
While rubber boots make their advance.
Chasing fits of giggling quirks,
As puddles give their playful jerks.

Faded Memories in Blurred Colors

Splat! A drop like jellybeans,
Faded dreams in squishy scenes.
Laughter echoes, skies in gray,
Where memories slip away.

Chasing rainbows, slipping shoes,
Finding joy in silly blues.
In this world, so wet and wild,
Every moment, a smiling child.

Serenading Hues in the Drench

Colors dance in puddles wide,
Bubbles popping, laughter cried.
Umbrellas flip, a wind-blown show,
Drenched, but look at us go!

Raincoats squeak, it's quite the sight,
Giggling folks with shoes so bright.
Kites are flying, or they try,
Chasing raindrops from the sky.

Splashing joy on gritty ground,
Each footfall makes a silly sound.
Dancing droplets, feet awake,
Wobbling, swinging, what a cake!

Puddles mirror our delight,
Jumps and twirls, a pure delight.
As we whirl in moisture's care,
Each raindrop sings, a concert fair.

Textured Harmony Under Raindrops

Woven tales on street we share,
Chatting, laughing without care.
Twisted rhythms in the spray,
Singing tunes to end the gray.

Rubber boots in bold display,
Kicking water, come what may.
We're the jesters of the storm,
Making mischief, breaking norm.

Colors clash on our parade,
Every splash a serenade.
Hats askew, a grand buffet,
Drenched delights lead us astray.

Carefree moments as we bounce,
Laughter shared with every flounce.
Songs of joy, oh what a spree,
In the downpour, wild and free!

Elegant Hangings of a Styled Storm

Raindrops smile upon our heads,
Each drop sprinkled where it treads.
Glistening hats in a range of hues,
Pardon us while we amuse!

Slipping, sliding, what a tour,
Dashing past like a running boar.
With each tumble and each slide,
We bring laughter as our guide.

Patterns formed in puddle fights,
An orchestra of joyous sights.
Hats doffed, we throw our hands,
And dance like joy's in high demands.

Each splatter, a note in play,
The weather’s whims can’t lead astray.
In a show of humors bright,
We twirl and leap—what pure delight!

Surreal Threads in a Melodic Downpour

Strings of laughter cross the street,
Puddles murmur beneath our feet.
Capes that flutter, colors spin,
We laugh as the rain rolls in.

Crazy hats form quite the scene,
Dancing puddles, shimmering sheen.
Feet that stomp in rhythm's beat,
We take the rain, we can’t be beat!

Whirls of water, a splash parade,
Each dribble tossed, a joyful spade.
Giggly while we brave the storm,
With every drop, we find our form.

Under clouds, we weave and play,
Turning gray to wacky spray.
As the thunder rolls and sways,
We keep our smiles, come what may!

A Symphony of Moisture and Style

When droplets dance on sleek, bright threads,
They twirl and sway, as if well-bred.
Witty hats tip, they catch a spray,
Chasing umbrellas that sneak away.

Puddles reflect a vibrant scene,
With splashes of joy, oh what a glean!
Fashion's a joke when the skies conspire,
To drench all the chic, oh what a pyre!

So let us prance in our wet attire,
With soggy shoes, we never tire.
Giggles escape as rain pours down,
What once was style, now a clown's crown!

In synchronized chaos, we bloom bright,
With waterlogged threads in full delight.
Give a nod to style that can’t withstand,
For humor reigns in this damp land.

Fragile Embroidery under Drizzles

Raindrops fall on soft pursuits,
Mocking the patterns, how they dilutes.
Frills get twisted, colors collide,
In this wet game, no room to hide!

Outfits sigh as puddles throw,
A splash of color in clad's flow.
When fabric wilts, laughter erupts,
As delicate art falls, corrupts!

Stitch by stitch, we waddle and weave,
Through puddles that mock what we believe.
Soaked in style, yet spirits remain,
Who knew that drizzles could entertain?

Adventurous threads take form anew,
Crafting a story of dark and blue.
With a sprinkle here and a twist of fate,
Watered fashion never feels late.

Accents in the Showering Light

Splashes of color in sunlight's embrace,
With every rainfall, a silly chase.
Hats spin wildly in wind's cheeky play,
As shoelaces laugh, come what may!

Giggling beads on jackets don't mind,
In puddles' dance, pure joy you'll find.
When warmth meets wet, the jokes ensue,
Bright accents drip, who knew they flew?

Puddles invite jigs and jests unheard,
Mismatched socks now the fashion bird.
With watercolor skies painting our feet,
Why not indulge in this soggy treat?

Raindrop symphonies at play with flair,
Married to laughter, we frolic with care.
Embrace the chaos of sunlight and rain,
For in every drop, we break the mundane.

Liquid Melodies of Soft Textiles

In the storm's embrace, we play along,
With cotton clouds, singing our song.
Threads shimmer bright, in the downpour's whirl,
Wrapped in whimsy, we giggle and twirl.

Satin shoes squelch with every bound,
Slippery frolics, joy unbound.
With each splash, we create our tunes,
Beneath the broad umbrella's moons!

Drenched but dapper, it's quite the feat,
Fashion's drowned, but not our beat.
Laughter rings out as the skies confide,
That style's just a frame for joy to ride!

In puddles' embrace, adore the mess,
Glee reigns supreme, no one to impress.
Liquid laughter beckons, come what may,
In the tender rain, we dance and sway.

Swaying Embers in a Hazy Mist

In the mist, we twist and turn,
Like dancers lost, we laugh and yearn.
A spark in puddles, oh what a sight,
We twirl through raindrops, a funny delight.

With every splash, our shoes take flight,
Who needs dry land when the world feels right?
We slip and slide, our giggles combine,
Dancing on sidewalks, just sipping moonshine.

Umbrellas turned inside out are the best,
Our fashion statement might just be a jest.
So here in the chaos, we let our hearts sway,
As mist wraps us gently in its playful ballet.

Oh, what’s that? A squishy old shoe!
Right in the puddle it says, 'We’re through!'
Yet laughter bursts forth, we don’t seem to care,
In this watery world, we float without a scare.

Echoes of Beauty Amidst Falling Water

Drops of joy dance on my head,
Each one whispers, 'Let go of dread.'
We march in the puddles, boots all aglow,
While thunder's our drummer, we steal the show.

The rain plays tricks, but we're well prepared,
Splashing in laughter, our worries ensnared.
We sing off-key while the clouds softly sigh,
In this drenched comedy, we're all flying high.

A squirrel in a slicker? What a sight to behold!
His tiny umbrella, looking bold yet cold.
We chuckle and chime, as the sky starts to clear,
What a funny twist in our waterlogged cheer!

Every droplet a note, we compose a tune,
Underneath the downpour, we dance with the moon.
The world turns glimmering, a comic ballet,
In this soggy symphony, come join our play!

Glimmering Edges of a Drenching Dream

Oh what a dream, swaddled in wet,
Puddles appear, our laughter's not set.
We slide through the streets on a water-slick floor,
Trying to dance, but we laugh wanting more.

A fish in a hurry, rushed on a quest,
Splashes a wave, he’s my new best guest.
With every step taken, my shoes squeak a song,
While the clouds tip their hats as they dance along.

We’re soaked to the bone, yet spirits take flight,
With every new droplet, we’re feeling just right.
So grab a wet napkin, let’s make this a feast,
As rain falls in rhythms, our fun has increased!

Through puddles we plod, each step a new tale,
Creating our circus on a watery trail.
Here in the splashes, our joy finds its beam,
Each curtain of water, a glimmering dream.

Draped in Softness as Clouds Weep

Clouds sob gently, but we're not so shy,
With umbrellas above, oh, how we fly!
Dancing in raindrops like nobody's game,
We skip through the downpour, no two steps the same.

A parade of splashes, we march to the beat,
In raincoats and laughter, life's oh-so-sweet.
Our shadows grow soggy, but who even cares?
With puddles like mirrors reflecting our stares!

Hats turned inside out, oh, what a mix!
Umbrellas like mushrooms, just pure little tricks.
As laughter erupts from our drippy embrace,
We watch as the world turns into a race.

With every drop falling, our spirits lift high,
As umbrellas take flight, just like a kite's sky.
In this dampened dance party, oh what a scene,
We twirl in the softness—what a funny routine!